W9-BVP-985

THE PHILIPPINES

by Bitsy Kemper

The Child's World

Published by The Child's World®
1980 Lookout Drive • Mankato, MN 56003-1705
800-599-READ • www.childsworld.com

Acknowledgments
The Child's World®: Mary Berendes, Publishing Director
Red Line Editorial: Editorial direction
The Design Lab: Design
Amnet: Production

Design elements: Shutterstock Images; Tristan Tan/
Shutterstock Images; Andrew Chin/Shutterstock Images
Photographs ©: Shutterstock Images, cover (left center), cover
(right), 1 (bottom left), 11, 17 (left), 21, 28; Tristan Tan/
Shutterstock Images, cover (left bottom), 1 (bottom right);
Andrew Chin/Shutterstock Images, cover (left top), 1 (top),
17 (right); iStockphoto, 5, 8, 9, 12, 19, 25, 27; Marcus
Lindstrom/iStockphoto, 6–7; Ed Stock/iStockphoto, 14;
Simon Gurney/iStockphoto, 15; Art Phaneuf/iStockphoto,
22, 26; Elena Yakusheva/Shutterstock Images, 24; Art
Phaneuf/Shutterstock Images, 30

ISBN 9781634070546
LCCN 2014959745

Printed in the United States of America
PA02353

ABOUT THE AUTHOR
Bitsy Kemper has written more than a dozen books. She's active in sports, church, and theater (but not all at the same time). Kemper loves a good laugh as much as a good read. Busy with three kids, she also enjoys learning about new cultures.

TABLE OF CONTENTS

ARCTIC
OCEAN

ATLANTIC
OCEAN

PACIFIC
OCEAN

INDIAN
OCEAN

PHILIPPINES
PACIFIC
OCEAN

SCALE

0   1000 Miles

0   1000 KM

N
W   E
S

SOUTHERN
OCEAN

PHILIPPINES

FUN FACT

ONE WORLD · MANY COUNTRIES

Pilipinas

10

The Philippines is about 600 miles (960 km) off the coast of Asia. It was given the nickname "Pearl of the Orient Sea" by the Filipino national hero José Rizal. He was a writer and poet. He also fought for the Philippines to be independent from Spain.

CHAPTER 1

WELCOME TO THE PHILIPPINES!

It is December. Giant star-shaped lanterns called *parols* hang in malls and streets. Some are 20 feet (6 m) tall, with blinking lights. The biggest are paraded around by truck. Cities sparkle and glow. Visitors come from all over to see the stars.

The lanterns stand for the Star of Bethlehem. Christians believe this star led people to Jesus more than 2,000 years ago. *Parols* represent hope to Filipinos. They are people who live in the Philippine Islands.

Parols decorate the streets of a small village in the Philippines.

The island nation of the Philippines is home to more than 100 million people. It includes more than 7,000 islands in the Pacific Ocean.

Their country has had struggles. Many people cannot afford homes so they live on the streets. To find jobs, some workers move to different countries and send money home. They are proud of their beautiful island home.

Filipino children

CHAPTER 2

THE LAND

Green mountaintops rise from the ocean near Busuanga Island.

The Philippines is a group of 7,107 islands. They are in the Pacific Ocean. The largest island is Luzon. It is in the northern part of the Philippines. Luzon makes up about one-third of the country's land. Mindanao is the second-largest island. It is in the southern part of the Philippines. People live on only about one-third of the islands. Most Filipinos live on Luzon or Mindanao.

Luzon, Mindanao, and the other islands have more than 22,548 miles (36,289 km) of coastline. The coastline has many beaches.

There are almost 100 mountains in the country. Among those mountains are many active volcanoes. During a storm in 1991, Luzon's Mount Pinatubo erupted. It spit ash, and the rainy winds carried the ash all over the islands.

It was one of the worst eruptions in modern history. It caused great damage to people and land. Air pollution spread around the world.

The crater left by Mount Pinatubo's eruption became a new lake.

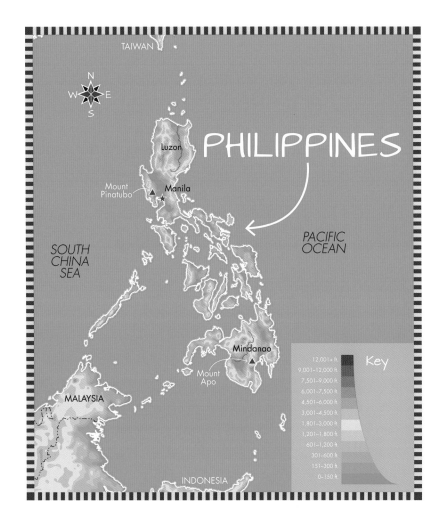

The country is known for nice weather all year. Most of the time, the weather is more than 80 degrees Fahrenheit (27°C). Sometimes the Philippines experiences **typhoons**. Typhoons begin over the ocean and then make their way to land. Homes are flooded and trees are knocked over.

The land offers many natural resources, such as nickel, iron, and copper. The soil is good for growing rice, corn, sugarcane, and coconuts.

The Philippines has more than 200 species of mammals, including chevrotains. These animals look like a mouse mixed with a deer. They are about 12 inches (30 cm) tall, and are active in the evening and at night.

FUN FACT • ONE WORLD, MANY COUNTRIES •

Pilipinas

CHAPTER 3

GOVERNMENT AND CITIES

People show their pride in the Philippines by waving flags.

The official name of the Philippines is the **Republic** of the Philippines. The country is divided into regions and provinces. They are similar to states. The regions and provinces are divided into *barangays*. Each has a local government.

PHILIPPINES

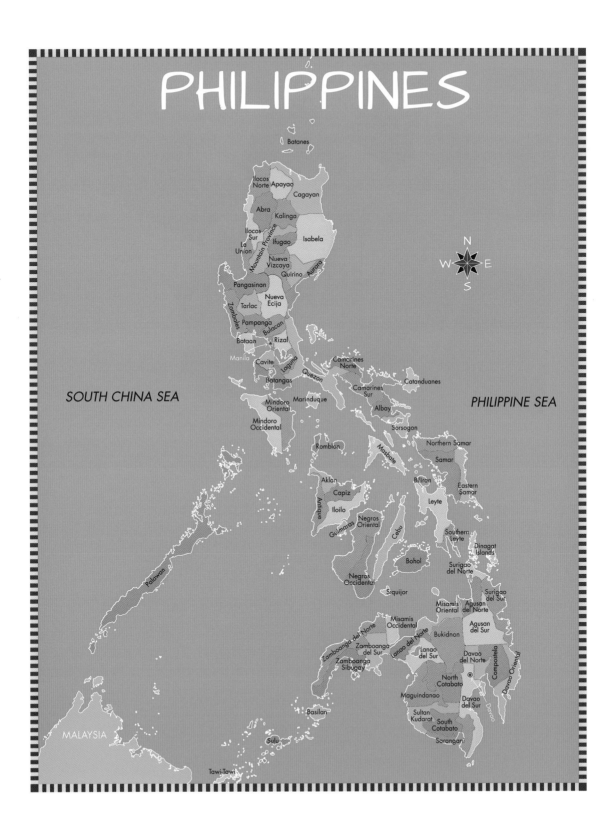

SOUTH CHINA SEA

PHILIPPINE SEA

MALAYSIA

Batanes

Ilocos Norte
Apayao
Cagayan
Abra
Kalinga
Ilocos Sur
Mountain Province
Ifugao
Isabela
La Union
Nueva Vizcaya
Quirino
Aurora
Pangasinan
Nueva Ecija
Zambales
Tarlac
Pampanga
Bulacan
Bataan
Rizal
Manila
Cavite
Laguna
Quezon
Batangas
Camarines Norte
Camarines Sur
Catanduanes
Mindoro Oriental
Marinduque
Albay
Mindoro Occidental
Sorsogon
Romblon
Northern Samar
Masbate
Samar
Aklan
Biliran
Eastern Samar
Capiz
Antique
Iloilo
Leyte
Guimaras
Negros Oriental
Southern Leyte
Cebu
Dinagat Islands
Bohol
Surigao del Norte
Palawan
Negros Occidental
Siquijor
Surigao del Sur
Misamis Oriental
Agusan del Norte
Misamis Occidental
Agusan del Sur
Zamboanga del Norte
Bukidnon
Zamboanga del Sur
Lanao del Norte
Compostela
Zamboanga Sibugay
Lanao del Sur
Davao del Norte
Davao Oriental
North Cotabato
Davao
Maguindanao
Davao del Sur
Basilan
Sultan Kudarat
South Cotabato
Sulu
Sorangani
Tawi-Tawi

A Filipino citizen fills out his ballot to vote for the president in 2010.

The national government of the Philippines is a republic. This means voters elect leaders to represent them in the government. The president leads the government. Lawmakers create laws in the Congress of the Philippines. Courts settle legal issues.

The national government meets in Manila. It is the capital of the Philippines. Manila is also the country's largest city. About 12 million people live there.

The Pasig River flows through Manila and drains into Manila Bay and then the South China Sea.

Manila is in the southern part of Luzon Island. It is crowded. About one of every ten Filipinos lives in or near Manila. It is a city of great variety. Skyscrapers stand next to 100-year-old buildings. Fast cars park next to horse-drawn carts.

The city of Davao has farmlands and hills. The country's largest mountain is there. Mount Apo is more than 9,600 feet (2,954 m) tall. It is one of the many active volcanoes. The national park that surrounds it has many animals and plants. The government protects the land and its wildlife.

Davao is alive with business and trading. It is a very diverse city, too. Davao is home to at least 11 native tribes. Christians and Muslims live there, too. The different cultures and religions blend different languages and lifestyles in the busy city.

Filipinos are working to improve their **economy**. In the past, people had few job choices. Many people had no jobs at all. Today, about 4 million Filipinos are jobless. They live in the streets or in shacks. More than half live on less than $2 a day.

This is slowly changing. As businesses grow, they create new jobs. The Philippines is now a major producer of electronics. Computers, toys, and cars all over the world use parts made and assembled by Filipinos.

Many Filipinos are also farmers. They grow fruit on their land. Banana farms alone create jobs for more than 200,000 Filipinos. Fruit is an important **export**.

The Philippines' currency

The Philippines' flag

FUN FACT

ONE WORLD · MANY COUNTRIES

When Ferdinand Magellan arrived in the Philippine islands, he named them *Islas de San Lazaro*. The name was later changed to the Philippines to honor Spain's King Philip II.

GLOBAL CONNECTIONS

In 1521, explorer Ferdinand Magellan landed in the Philippine islands. People, mostly from Asia, already lived there. He claimed the islands for Spain. The Philippines stayed under Spanish rule for the next 300 years.

During that time, Filipinos adopted many Spanish customs. The Spanish added math and business to schools. They built colleges. Spanish words became part of everyday language. Many native Filipinos had to take Spanish last names.

In the late 1800s, the United States took control. Volunteers came in to teach. Americans added the English language to schools, which became free to attend. American items such as tennis shoes and bubble gum became popular. Filipinos adopted English words, such as *keyk* for cake. The islands followed U.S. law until they became independent in 1946.

CHAPTER 4

PEOPLE AND CULTURES

The Philippines has a growing population. More than 100 million people live on the islands. Most Filipinos have **ancestors** from Malaysia, Indonesia, and China. Many can also trace their roots back to Spain and the United States.

Filipino families can trace their roots back to many parts of Asia.

The islands have almost 100 **ethnic** groups. There are also people who have **immigrated**. They come from Vietnam, Taiwan, India, Japan, Korea, Europe, and the United States.

More than 170 languages are spoken in the Philippines. Two of those languages are official. They are English and Filipino. English became widely spoken after U.S. rule of the country in the 1900s. Filipino is based on Tagalog. It comes from the island's Tagalog ethnic group.

Respecting elders is important in the Philippines. Elders are addressed with word "po" added to the end of a sentence. Friends would use the word *salamat* to say "thank you" to each other. If talking to a grandparent, that same person would use the words *salamat po* to say "thank you." It is a way of showing respect.

Filipinos use other signs of respect, too. When younger family members greet an elder, they may kiss the elder's hand. Or they may place the hand of the elder on their foreheads. These are special acts of honor.

The Philippines is the only nation in Asia that is mostly Christian. Approximately 80 percent of the country is Roman

This Filipino man is wearing traditional clothing from the Ifugao province.

Catholics on Leyte Island attend a Sunday church service.

Catholic. There are people of other faiths, too. Muslims make up 5 percent of the population.

Many holidays are Christian, such as Christmas. The Christmas season stretches from September to January. On Christmas Eve, *Noche Buena*, many people attend church at midnight. Everyone looks forward to a big family dinner afterward. On Christmas morning, people open gifts. When they visit their grandparents or other relatives, they get fresh bills of money called *aginaldo*.

Another religious holiday is *Flores de Mayo*. The month-long festival honors Mary, the mother of Jesus in the Bible. Girls dress up in their finest clothes. They bring flowers to churches. The festival ends with a large parade. Images of Mary on bamboo poles are carried through the streets. Bundles of coins and food hang from the poles.

CHAPTER 5

DAILY LIFE

Girls sit on the steps of a bamboo house, making toys from leaves.

Before Spanish settlers arrived, Filipino families lived in simple homes. The one-room homes were made of wood or bamboo and rested on stilts. Soon homes were made of brick. Second stories were added. They looked like homes from Spain.

Today many in the countryside live in *bahay kubos*. The simple buildings have windows without glass. This allows fresh air to blow through the houses. The insides are also simple, with little furniture.

Elsewhere, homes range from basic huts to modern two-story homes. With many poor people, crowded cities have tiny shacks where family members live together in one room.

The national dish of the Philippines is *adobo*. It is meat or seafood that has been cooked in soy sauce, vinegar, and garlic. It is often served with white rice.

A traditional Filipino home on Coron Island

Cooks prepare food at a street cart. Common street foods include fried fish balls and grilled meats.

Meals are not made for one person. Many people from the same family live under one roof. Grandparents live with their children and grandchildren.

People in the Philippines mostly wear modern, casual clothes. Sometimes Filipinos choose to wear traditional clothing. For men, this is a *barong tagalog*. It is a dressy, white shirt that is worn untucked. The traditional clothing for women is a *baro't saya*. It is a long skirt and a shirt. Dressing in white dates back to the original Philippine people more than

500 years ago, when the common man wore a simple white cotton top.

Muslims in southern Mindanao might wear colorful *malongs*. A *malong* is a large cloth wrapped around the body. Both men and women wear it.

Cars, buses, and trains are used around the country. Horse-drawn carriages are used, too. Three-wheeled carts carry people across town. Bicycles and motorcycles work well in crowded cities and on country roads.

Filipino women wear *baro't sayas* to celebrate Independence Day.

"Jeepneys" are popular buses. They are made from the jeeps left behind by U.S. soldiers. With many colors and decorations, they are easy to spot.

FUN FACT

Pilipinas

10₱

ONE WORLD · MANY COUNTRIES ·

Between islands, some travel by boat. *Bancas* are wooden boats that have been used for hundreds of years. They seat a few people at a time. More modern versions are made from metal. They can carry up to 50 people.

Over the years, life in the Philippines has been hard. Foreign rulers affected the country in different ways. They also added to the country's diverse culture. The country continues to grow. Its people look forward to a bright future.

DAILY LIFE FOR CHILDREN

The Philippine school year runs from June to March. Children attend school from 7:30 in the morning until 4:30 or 5:00 in the afternoon. School is free. It is also the law. Children from ages seven to 12 must attend.

Playing outside is much more common than playing indoors with electronics. One common game is *patintero,* which is like tag. *Luksong baka* is like leapfrog. *Piko* is like hopscotch.

People speak many languages throughout the country. Public schools teach in the local language for the first two years. English and Filipino are taught after that. High schools and colleges mostly use English.

FAST FACTS

Population: 107 million

Area: 115,830 square miles (300,000 sq km)

Capitol: Manila

Largest Cities: Manila and Davao

Form of Government: Republic

Languages: Filipino (also called Tagalog) and English

Trading Partners: Japan, United States, and China

Major Holidays: Christmas, Philippine Independence Day, National Heroes Day

National Dish: Adobo (meat stewed in vinegar and garlic)

Filipino children relax outside after school.

GLOSSARY

ancestors (AN-sess-turz) Ancestors are people who were part of a family many years ago. Many Filipinos have ancestors from Malaysia, Indonesia, and China.

economy (ih-KON-uh-me) An economy is how a country runs its industry, trade, and finance. The economy in the Philippines is growing.

ethnic (ETH-nik) Ethnic describes a group with a common language, culture, religion, or background. The Philippines has many ethnic groups.

export (ek-SPORT) To export means to sell goods to another country. The Philippines exports goods to other countries.

immigrated (IM-ih-grated) Immigrated refers to people who moved to another country to live. Many people in the Philippines have immigrated.

republic (ree-PUB-lick) A republic is a place where an elected official rules over the land and people. The Philippines is a republic.

typhoons (tie-FOONS) Typhoons are storms that bring strong winds and heavy rains. Typhoons are a danger in the Philippines.

TO LEARN MORE

BOOKS

Capistrano, Tricia J. *Dingding, Ningning, Singsing and Other Fun Tagalog Words*. Tricia J. Capistrano, 2012.

Romulo, Liana. *Filipino Celebrations: A Treasury of Feasts and Festivals*. North Clarendon, VT: Tuttle Publishing, 2012.

WEB SITES

Visit our Web site for links about the Philippines:
childsworld.com/links

Note to Parents, Teachers, and Librarians: We routinely verify our Web links to make sure they are safe and active sites. So encourage your readers to check them out!

INDEX